ALTERNATOR BOOKS™

INSIDE ALCATRAZ

TOP SECRET

HEATHER E. SCHWARTZ

Lerner Publications ◆ Minneapolis

Lerner Publications Company
An imprint of Lerner Publishing Group, Inc.
241 First Avenue North
Minneapolis, MN 55401 USA

For reading levels and more information, look up this title at www.lernerbooks.com.

Main body text set in Aptifer Sans LT Pro.
Typeface provided by Linotype AG.

Editor: Lauren Foley **Designer:** Athena Currier

Library of Congress Cataloging-in-Publication Data

Names: Schwartz, Heather E., author.
Title: Inside Alcatraz / Heather E. Schwartz.
Description: Minneapolis, MN : Lerner Publications, [2023] | Series: Top secret (Alternator Books) | Includes bibliographical references and index. | Audience: Ages 8–12 | Audience: Grades 4–6 | Summary: "Attempted escapes, suspected paranormal activity, and more mark Alcatraz's history. Dive deep into Alcatraz and find out how it's become a popular spot for history buffs and ghost hunters alike"— Provided by publisher.
Identifiers: LCCN 2022017722 (print) | LCCN 2022017723 (ebook) | ISBN 9781728476605 (library binding) | ISBN 9781728478319 (paperback) | ISBN 9781728485300 (ebook)
Subjects: LCSH: United States Penitentiary, Alcatraz Island, California—History—Juvenile literature. | Prisons—California—Alcatraz Island—History—Juvenile literature. | Alcatraz Island (Calif.)—History—Juvenile literature.
Classification: LCC HV9474.A4 S39 2023 (print) | LCC HV9474.A4 (ebook) | DDC 365/.979461—dc23/eng/20220701

LC record available at https://lccn.loc.gov/2022017722
LC ebook record available at https://lccn.loc.gov/2022017723

Manufactured in the United States of America
1-52241-50681-7/12/2022

TABLE OF CONTENTS

INTRODUCTION

INMATES ON THE LOOSE

On June 12, 1962, guards walked through Alcatraz Federal Penitentiary to check that all the prisoners were in their beds. They discovered three beds held dummy heads made of plaster, with painted faces and real human hair. The dummies were so lifelike that they'd fooled guards throughout the night. But by morning, it was clear that inmates Frank Morris, John Anglin, and Clarence Anglin were missing.

But where could they have gone? Alcatraz is built on an island of the same name in the San Francisco Bay, California. It is surrounded by more than 1 mile (1.6 km)

SUBJECT:

of freezing water with dangerous currents. Prisoners had no hope of escape. Yet no one could find Morris and the Anglin brothers. And no one ever would.

The cold waters of the San Francisco Bay surround Alcatraz.

CHAPTER 1
NO WAY OUT

The lighthouse on Alcatraz helps ships navigate the bay and avoid the island.

Alcatraz is filled with cells from its time as a military and, later, federal prison.

Before the US took control of Alcatraz Island in 1848, it was a wildlife habitat. Thousands of nesting birds made their home on the rocky island. But the peaceful spot soon had darker uses. It first became a military fort, then later a military prison. By 1933, the US Army didn't need the prison anymore. The federal government took over. Alcatraz became a prison for the country's worst criminals.

Some Alcatraz cells had small desks.

Life on the Rock

Even hardened criminals knew Alcatraz was a terrible place to be. It had high security, and prisoners got few privileges they could enjoy. Mostly, they had only the basics: food, clothing, shelter, and medicine. And the Rock, as it was nicknamed, was packed with dangerous convicts.

Despite the rough conditions, some convicts wanted to go to Alcatraz. They knew they'd get hot showers because officials didn't want them to get used to cold water that felt like the ocean. Prisoners also knew they'd have their own cell. But the tiny space was far from cushy. Lit by a bare bulb, each cell held a toilet, sink, and a thin mattress on a steel bed frame against a concrete wall.

Escape Attempts

Single cells made it easy for guards to keep a close eye on prisoners. An empty cell meant someone was missing. That was why many prisoners wound up on the Rock. They had a history of escape attempts. Morris and the Anglin brothers had even met at a prison in Atlanta that the brothers later tried to escape from. But officials were certain they'd be secure at Alcatraz, a place no prisoner had ever been proven to escape and survive.

SOLVE IT

In 1937, convicted bank robbers Theodore Cole and Ralph Roe broke out of Alcatraz by sawing through the bars on a window. When no one could find them, officials decided they'd drowned in the bay. But people reported sightings of the two men for years. Do you think the men survived? How would you find out? You could start by researching the escape or interviewing people who know about the case.

Rough, cold waves in the San Francisco Bay

Even though escape seemed impossible, many prisoners still tried. Fourteen attempts were made between 1934 and 1963. Runaway prisoners who made it to the ocean faced dangerous challenges. Fast currents could pull weak, untrained swimmers under. And the extremely cold water could easily cause hypothermia and death.

Most escapees were caught. Six were shot. Two drowned. But a few disappeared. Was it possible they made it to the mainland?

CHAPTER 2

MYSTERIOUSLY MISSING

An old sign for the prison is now displayed inside.

The Alcatraz library used to be filled with books for prisoners to read.

Life at Alcatraz could get boring. Prisoners had to earn privileges that might make the days go by faster. They could earn the right to work in places like the prison barbershop, write letters to family, visit the prison library, paint, and play music. Many prisoners fell in line so they could enjoy these privileges.

A concertina

In 1962, Morris had earned music privileges and received a small accordion called a concertina that he could use during music hour. One of the Anglin brothers earned a job in the prison barbershop. Another inmate they knew, Leon "Whitey" Thompson, took up oil painting.

Although it looked as though the inmates were adjusting to life at Alcatraz, Morris had other ideas. Each privilege he and his friends earned became part of his plans.

Plotting and Scheming

Another inmate, Allen West, planned to cut through the ceiling air vent to the roof. Other inmates joined the plot. The group worked for eight months. They stole saw blades, dug through cell walls, and created the dummy heads. The privileges they earned came in handy as they worked. Thompson helped them blend paint to create a skin tone for the dummies. Scraps of human hair were easy to swipe from the barbershop.

Real hair and paint made the dummy heads look more lifelike.

They also built a raft and paddles to navigate the bay. They made life preservers out of raincoats from other prisoners. Morris took apart his concertina to create a bellows to inflate the raft. They also planned to steal a car and clothing on the mainland.

The men hid their efforts from the guards. They dug during music hour so the sounds would be masked. They covered up the holes they made with painted cardboard.

On June 11, 1962, Morris, West, and the Anglin brothers put their plan into action. First each had to escape from his cell. That's where things went wrong for West. He'd used cement to secure a vent covering the hole he needed to get through.

From left to right: Clarence Anglin, John Anglin, and Frank Morris

Morris and the Anglins escaped through the vents in their cells.

But the cement had hardened. He was trapped and couldn't leave with the others.

Morris and the Anglin brothers had to move fast to save themselves. They escaped through the air vents they'd dug open in their cells, met in the hall, and climbed up pipes to the ceiling. When they reached the hole they'd cut to the roof, they climbed through and exited the prison.

As soon as guards realized the men were missing, the FBI was called. They interviewed West and other inmates who knew about the plan. They learned what had happened. But it was too late to stop Morris and the Anglin brothers. The inmates were officially missing.

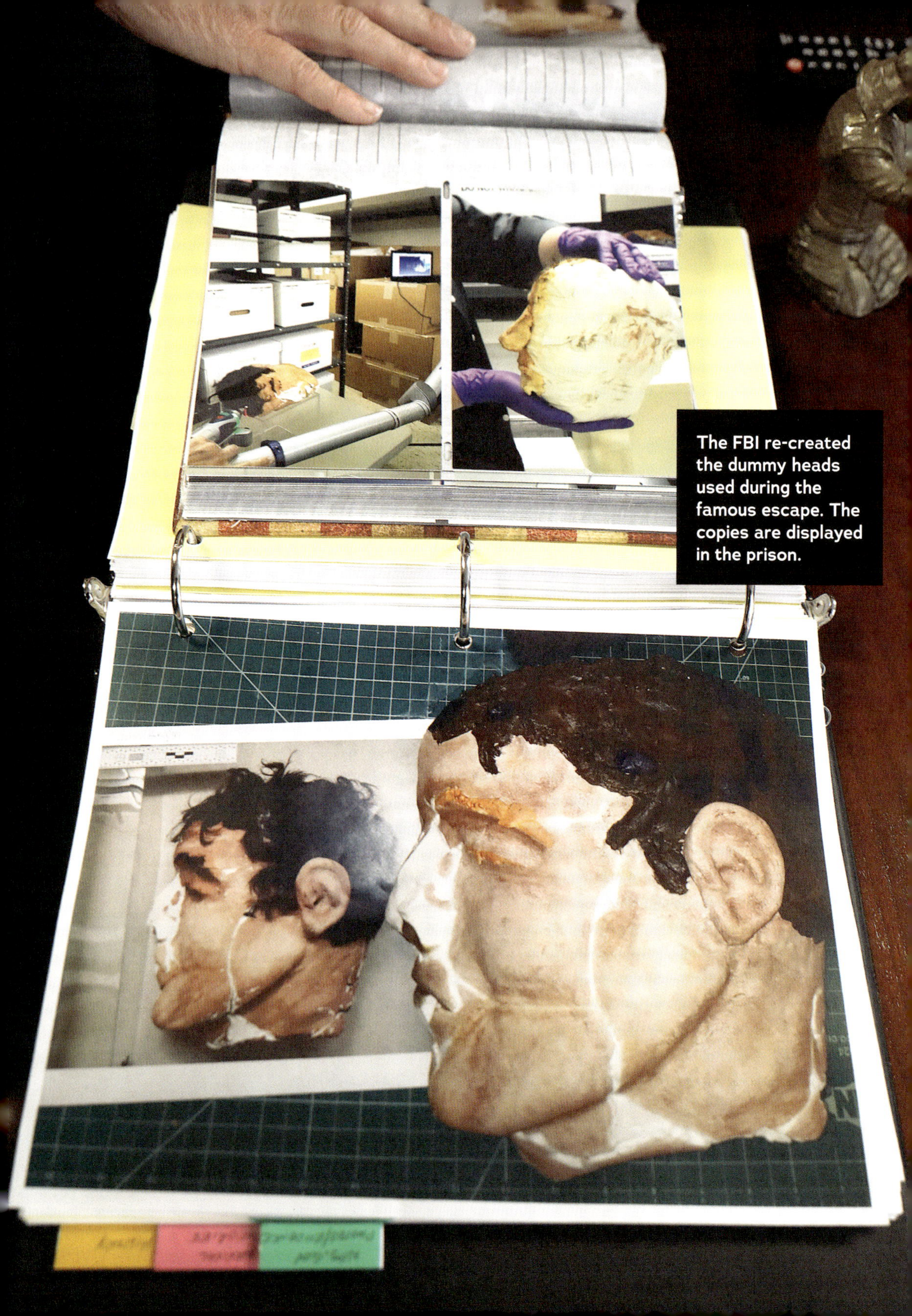

The FBI re-created the dummy heads used during the famous escape. The copies are displayed in the prison.

DECLASSIFIED

Evidence showed that Morris and the Anglin brothers made it to the water with their raft. Did they paddle to the mainland and live the rest of their lives free? The FBI examined several clues. It seemed unlikely the escapees could have survived the cold water and strong currents in the bay. There was no evidence they'd had help from family or stolen a car and clothing on the mainland as they'd planned. The FBI determined the men died in their attempt to escape Alcatraz.

The FBI case was closed on December 31, 1979. But it's still under investigation by the US Marshals Service. Why? Because the mystery wasn't really solved. Without evidence to prove the men died, it is possible at least one of them survived.

Celebrity Criminals

The story of the attempted escape caught the nation's imagination. Author J. Campbell Bruce wrote about it in his 1963 book *Escape from Alcatraz*. His chapters about Morris and the Anglin brothers were later made into a movie.

Alcatraz had many other well-known inmates. Gangster Al Capone ran a violent crime ring in Chicago before arriving at the prison in 1934. He was ill, which may explain why he quietly followed most of the rules. But Capone spoke

Al Capone was one of Alcatraz's most famous inmates.

Robert Stroud was nicknamed the Birdman of Alcatraz.

up about one passion. He wanted to start a prison band. Eventually guards allowed it. He learned guitar, banjo, and mandola. Capone played with other inmates in a band called the Rock Islanders.

Convicted murderer Robert Stroud arrived in 1942. Stroud had used his time in other prisons to study birds. But guards eventually found he was up to no good. He hid contraband in birdcages. He requested special equipment for the birds, then used it to make alcohol. His bad behavior got him transferred to the Rock, where he was known as the Birdman of Alcatraz.

CHAPTER 3

GHOST STORIES

The outside of Alcatraz prison at night

Over a mile (1.6 km) away from the mainland, Alcatraz Island is quiet and isolated.

Prisoners who couldn't escape Alcatraz had little relief from watchful guards, a dull daily schedule, and the promise of punishment if they stepped out of line. Many of them lay awake at night with their minds racing. They were sure they heard laughter on the mainland, more than a mile (1.6 km) away.

Open for Tours

Alcatraz kept prisoners in line, but it was expensive to run. Its costs were so high that it closed as a prison in 1963. By the time it closed, almost sixteen hundred men had served time on the island. The location became a tourist attraction in 1973. But guards still work there at night. And they've reported strange sounds and eerie sightings that suggest the living aren't the only visitors.

Imagine walking the empty halls of the prison with only a flashlight and a gun for protection. Both would be

SOLVE IT

Alcatraz guards lived on the island with their families. But many inmates were convinced the sounds they heard at night came from farther away. Did it echo from the mainland? Some people also report hearing ghostly sounds at Alcatraz. Could the laughter have been paranormal? To find out where the sounds came from, you could try researching things like how far an echo can travel or how many families lived on the island.

D Block is said to be the most haunted cell block in Alcatraz. Inmates there were completely isolated.

useless against ghosts. And several guards say they have encountered them.

One guard who was on the night shift alone in the early 2000s heard glasses clinking together. He heard creepy laughter he hoped was just the wind. To calm his mind, he tried watching horror movies in Capone's former cell. The idea backfired, leaving him even more terrified as he patrolled the desolate prison.

Another night guard on duty after Alcatraz closed felt nervous entering the prison's electroshock therapy room. One night, he used a camera to take a picture of the

Some say Capone's banjo still echoes in the shower room.

empty space for his friends. At the time, the film had to be professionally developed before he could show them his photo. When it was ready, he was the one who got a shock. A face appeared in the picture that he hadn't seen when he was there in person.

It's scary enough to see and hear signs of ghosts when you're patrolling an empty prison. But one Alcatraz guard who worked nights says she was often pinched by what felt like human fingers. She couldn't think of a natural explanation. But could it have been supernatural?

By 2013, more than 1.4 million tourists were visiting Alcatraz each year. By 2019, numbers reached 1.6 million.

People can take tours through Alcatraz during the day and at night.

Even in 2022, many people were interested in tours that explored the former prison at night. On these tours, guides take visitors through the dark cell blocks. Visitors might hear ghostly screaming, crying, and moaning. But they might also encounter less scary ghostly activity. Some people say they can still hear Capone practicing his banjo in the shower room.

While Alcatraz is said to be filled with ghosts, three inmates are missing from these stories. No one ever found the bodies of Morris and the Anglin brothers. There haven't been reports of them haunting the island either. We know these men attempted a daring and likely impossible escape. But like much of Alcatraz's history, their fates remain a mystery.

Timeline

1848: The US takes control of Alcatraz Island.

1933: Alcatraz becomes a federal prison.

1934: Gangster Al Capone is sent to Alcatraz to serve his sentence.

1937: Convicted bank robbers Theodore Cole and Ralph Roe break out of Alcatraz.

1942: The Birdman of Alcatraz arrives on the island.

1962: Frank Morris, John Anglin, and Clarence Anglin escape from Alcatraz.

1963: Alcatraz is closed as a prison.

1969: A group of Indigenous people camp on Alcatraz as a protest. They claim the island as Indigenous land under the 1868 Treaty of Fort Laramie. The protest lasts for nineteen months.

1979: The FBI closes the case of Morris and the Anglin brothers.

2019: Alcatraz claims 1.6 million visitors.

Glossary

bellows: a device that produces a strong current of air when its sides are pressed together

contraband: things that are illegal for a prisoner to have

convict: a person serving a long sentence for a crime

desolate: lacking the people, plants, animals, and other things that make people feel welcome in a place

developed: when film has had chemicals applied to it to make images appear

electroshock therapy: a treatment for mental illness that uses electric current

hypothermia: a condition in which the temperature of the body is extremely low

mandola: a stringed musical instrument

paranormal: very strange and not able to be explained by what scientists know about nature and the world

privilege: a right or benefit that is given to some people and not to others

supernatural: things that cannot be explained by science and seem to involve magic or invisible agents such as ghosts or spirits

Learn More

Alcatraz Island Facts & History
https://easyscienceforkids.com/alcatraz-facts/

Alcatraz Island Facts for Kids
https://kids.kiddle.co/Alcatraz_Island

Britannica Kids: Alcatraz Island
https://kids.britannica.com/kids/article/Alcatraz/626495

Loh-Hagan, Virginia. *Alcatraz*. Ann Arbor, MI: Cherry Lake, 2021.

Morrison, Marie. *Alcatraz Is Haunted!* New York: PowerKids, 2020.

National Park Service: Alcatraz Island
https://www.nps.gov/alca/index.htm

Smith, Emma Bland. *The Gardener of Alcatraz: A True Story.* Watertown, MA: Charlesbridge, 2022.

Sullivan, Tom. *Jailbreak at Alcatraz: Frank Morris & the Anglin Brothers' Great Escape.* New York: Balzer + Bray, 2021.

Index

Photo Acknowledgments

Image credits: Benny Marty/Shutterstock, p. 1; EricFerguson/Getty Images, p. 5; eyfoto/Getty Images, p. 6; Jeff Whyte/Shutterstock, p. 7; Gennadii Borodin/Shutterstock, p. 8; Nick Starichenko/Shutterstock, p. 10; Geri Lavrov/Getty Images, p. 12; Jessica Bauman/Shutterstock, p. 13; cristianl/Getty Images, p. 14; Dharvey8259/Wikimedia Commons (CC BY-SA 4.0), p. 15; Bettmann/Getty Images, p. 16; Orange Grove/Shutterstock, p. 17; Liz Hafalia/The San Francisco Chronicle/Getty Images, p. 18; AP Photo/File, p. 20; American Stock Archive/Getty Images, p. 21; Ramin Talaie/Corbis/Getty Images, p. 22; Pung/Shutterstock, p. 23; Idealphotographer/Shutterstock, p. 25; Anne-Marie Hartman/Shutterstock, p. 26; Robert Alexander/Getty Images, p. 27.

Design elements: Ivan Gromov/Unsplash; Marjan Blan/Unsplash; fotograzia/Getty Images; Reddavebatcave/Shutterstock; AVS-Images/Shutterstock.

Cover: Sawasdee Snap/Shutterstock.